Cool Sports Facts

Cool Baseball Facts

by Kathryn Clay

Consulting Editor: Gail Saunders-Smith, PhD

Consultant: Craig Coenen, PhD
Associate Professor of History
Mercer County Community College
West Windsor, New Jersey

CAPSTONE PRESS
a capstone imprint

Pebble Plus is published by Capstone Press,
151 Good Counsel Drive, P.O. Box 669, Mankato, Minnesota 56002.
www.capstonepub.com

Books published by Capstone Press are manufactured with paper
containing at least 10 percent post-consumer waste.

Library of Congress Cataloging-in-Publication Data
Clay, Kathryn.
  Cool baseball facts / by Kathryn Clay.
    p. cm.—(Pebble plus. Cool sports facts)
  Includes bibliographical references and index.
  Summary: "Simple text and full-color photos illustrate facts about the rules, equipment, and records of baseball"—
Provided by publisher.
  ISBN 978-1-4296-4477-8 (library binding)
  1. Baseball—Miscellanea—Juvenile literature. I. Title. II. Series.
  GV867.5.C53 2011
  796.357—dc22   2009051408

Editorial Credits
Erika L. Shores, editor; Kyle Grenz, designer; Eric Gohl, media researcher; Eric Manske, production specialist

Photo Credits
AP Images/Chris O'Meara, 7; Richard Lui, 5
Corbis/Reuters/Sam Mircovich, 17
Dreamstime/Lawrence Weslowski Jr., cover
Getty Images Inc./Pool, 21; Sports Imagery/Ronald C. Modra, 19
The Granger Collection, New York, 9
MLB Photos via Getty Images/Arizona Diamondbacks/Jonathan Willey, 11; Rich Pilling, 15
Shutterstock/Adrian Coroama, cover (baseball), back cover, 1; Ken Inness, 13

The author dedicates this book to her dad, a lifelong Minnesota Twins fan.

Note to Parents and Teachers

The Cool Sports Facts series supports national social studies standards related to people, places,
and culture. This book describes and illustrates baseball. The images support early readers
in understanding the text. The repetition of words and phrases helps early readers learn new
words. This book also introduces early readers to subject-specific vocabulary words, which are
defined in the Glossary section. Early readers may need assistance to read some words and to
use the Table of Contents, Glossary, Read More, Internet Sites, and Index sections of the book.

Printed in the United States of America in North Mankato, Minnesota.
122010   006032R

Table of Contents

Home Run!

More than 70 million fans go to MLB games each year. These fans eat 30 million hot dogs while watching their favorite teams.

MLB stands for Major League Baseball.

Cool Equipment

Baseballs are rubbed

with mud before games.

It makes the balls

easier to throw.

The first official uniform
was worn in 1849.
The Knickerbockers wore
blue pants, white shirts,
and straw hats.

Cool Rules

Batters don't always need
to hit the ball to reach base.
Getting hit by a pitch sends
the batter to first.

It's against the rules

for a pitcher to spit on the ball.

A pitcher also can't rub

a ball on his glove or clothing.

Cool Records

In his career, Nolan Ryan
pitched seven games
without giving up a hit.
No other pitcher has thrown
as many no-hitters.

Only one player has ever

hit two grand slams

in the same inning.

Fernando Tatis did it

on April 23, 1999.

Baltimore Orioles shortstop
Cal Ripken Jr., didn't miss
a game in 16 years.
He played 2,632 games
in a row.

The New York Yankees

have won 27 World Series.

The St. Louis Cardinals have

the second most titles with 10.

Glossary

batter—the person whose turn it is to bat

grand slam—to hit a home run when there is a runner on every base

inning—part of a baseball game when each team gets a turn to bat; a baseball game has nine innings

no-hitter—a game in which no batter gets on base by hitting the ball; a batter can reach base in a no-hitter by walking or if the other team makes an error

pitch—a baseball thrown to the batter

shortstop—the position between second and third base

Read More

Franks, Katie. *I Want to Be a Baseball Player.* Dream Jobs. New York: PowerKids Press, 2007.

Kalman, Bobbie, and John Crossingham. *Batter Up Baseball*. Sports Starters. New York: Crabtree Pub. Company, 2007.

Internet Sites

FactHound offers a safe, fun way to find Internet sites related to this book. All of the sites on FactHound have been researched by our staff.

Here's all you do:

Visit *www.facthound.com*

FactHound will fetch the best sites for you!

Index

Word Count: 182

Grade: 1

Early-Intervention Level: 20